Tornado

BETSY BYARS

Tornado

illustrations by Doron Ben-Ami

HarperTrophy®
An Imprint of HarperCollinsPublishers

Harper Trophy® is a registered trademark of
HarperCollins Publishers Inc.

Tornado
Text copyright © 1996 by Betsy C. Byars
Illustrations copyright © 1996 by Doron Ben-Ami

Library of Congress Cataloging-in-Publication Data
Byars, Betsy Cromer.
    Tornado / by Betsy Byars ; illustrations by Doron Ben-Ami.
        p. cm.
    Summary: As they wait out a tornado in their storm cellar, a family
listens to their farmhand tells stories about the dog that was blown into
his life by another tornado when he was a boy.
    ISBN 0-06-026452-7 (lib. bdg.) — ISBN 0-06-442063-9 (pbk.)
    [1. Dogs — Fiction. 2. Tornadoes — Fiction.] I. Ben-Ami, Doron, ill.
II. Title.
PZ7.B9836To 1996   95-41584
[Fic] — dc20   CIP
                                                                AC

Typography by Gregory G. Jüng

First Harper Trophy edition, 1997
Revised Harper Trophy edition, 2004
Visit us on the World Wide Web!
www.harperchildrens.com

16 OPM 60 59 58 57

For the Giltners—
especially Zsa and Joe and Nine-Thirty

Contents

Tornado

CHAPTER 1
The Storm

"Twister!" Pete yelled. "Twister!"

I ran for the house.

"Twister!"

He pointed.

I looked over my shoulder. I could see it—a long, black funnel cloud in the west. It pointed from the dark sky right down to our farm.

Pete opened the doors to the storm cellar and beckoned with his straw hat.

"Twister!" he shouted again.

My two brothers ran from the barn. Pete helped my grandmother down the steps.

"Hurry up, boys," she called. Then she said to my mother, "Come on, Beth."

My mother was standing outside the door. She was worried about my daddy.

"Link! Link!" she called. My daddy had been named for a president. "Lincoln!"

"He's in the cornfield," Pete said. "He can't hear you, ma'am."

Still my mother hesitated. The cornfield seemed to be directly under the funnel.

"He'll be all right. He can get in a ditch. You come on now."

She ducked into the cellar, and Pete pulled the doors shut behind her.

The storm cellar was dim and cool. It smelled of potatoes and pickles. My mother kept sacks of root vegetables here along with boxes of eggs and jars of tomatoes.

My brothers and I sat on the dirt floor. My grandmother sat on a pickle barrel and my mother on an orange crate.

We sat for a moment, silent. We listened to the storm and worried about my father in the cornfield.

Something that sounded like gravel was thrown against the cellar doors.

"Hail," my mother said, and bowed her head.

Pete cleared his throat. "You know what this brings to my mind?" he said.

We knew, and my brothers and I

turned to him gratefully. We saw a flash of teeth as he smiled at us.

"It brings to mind a dog I had one time."

"Tornado," my brothers and I said together.

"How'd you know his name?" he teased. "Yes, I did call my dog Tornado."

Pete settled his straw hat on his head and began. "I remember it was an August day, a whole lot like this one."

CHAPTER 2

In the Doghouse

At breakfast that morning, I remember my mother looked up from the stove, took a breath, and said, "I smell a storm."

I shivered a little, because my mother's nose was always right.

My daddy said, "Well, you kids better stay close to the house."

The morning went by, slow and scary. We did stay close to the house. Folks didn't call our part of the country *Tornado Alley* for nothing.

Along about lunch, it hit. Only there was no warning like we had today. No funnel cloud, no nothing. One minute we were eating beans and biscuits at the table. Next there was a roar—worse than a train— worse than a hundred trains. And then there came a terrible tearing sound, like the world was being ripped apart. I can still hear it in my mind.

I looked up, and I saw sky. The ceiling was clean gone. There was the sky! The tornado had torn the roof off the kitchen and left the food on the table and us in our seats.

My daddy was the first to be able to speak. He said, "Well, I'm surprised to find myself alive."

That was how we all felt. We looked at our arms and legs to make sure they were still hooked on us.

Then my father pushed back his chair and said, "Let's go see the damage."

Outside, the yard was not our yard anymore. The tree with the tire swing was laid flat. The tops of all the pine trees had been snapped off. A doghouse I had never seen before was beside the well. A piece of bicycle was here, the hood of a car there. I stepped over somebody's clothesline that still had some clothes on it.

The roof of the kitchen lay at the edge of the garden. It was folded shut like a book. We walked over there.

"It was about time for a new roof," my daddy said. He always tried to find the good in something.

I was just walking around, looking

at other people's things, when I heard a rattling noise.

I kept listening and looking, and finally I realized the sound was coming from that doghouse. I went over to it.

The doghouse was trembling. You could see it. It was trembling. It was shaking. It was doing everything but having a fit.

I looked inside, and there was a big black dog. He was panting so hard, I could feel his breath. He was shaking so hard, the doghouse was in danger of losing its boards.

"Daddy, there's a dog in here!"

My daddy came over.

"Look, Daddy. It's a big black dog."

My daddy leaned down and took a look.

"Well, you can come on out now," he told the dog. "The storm's over, and you're among friends."

The dog just kept shaking.

"Maybe I can pull him out," I said.

"Don't you put your hand in there," my mother said.

"Yes, leave him be, Pete."

All that day, all that night, all the next day that dog shook. I brought him water, but he wouldn't drink. I brought him food, but he wouldn't eat.

Then that night my mother leaned out the kitchen door and yelled, "Supper!" as she usually did. The dog heard her and stuck his head out of the doghouse. He must have been familiar with the word.

He came out, stood there, looked

around for a moment, and then gave one final shake, as if he were shaking off the past. Then he came over and joined us at the back door.

I said, "Daddy, can we keep him? Please?"

"If we don't find the owner."

"Can we call him Tornado?"

"Until we find the owner."

"We'll have to ask around," my mother reminded me.

"I know."

My daddy bent down. "Let's see what kind of manners you got, Tornado. Shake!"

My daddy put out his hand. Tornado put out his paw. They shook like two men striking a bargain.

Then we all went in to supper.

CHAPTER 3

A Card Trick

"Speaking of Tornado," Pete went on, raising his voice over the sound of the wind, "reminds me of something funny that happened one time."

He waited, as if for encouragement.

"Is it about the three of hearts?" I asked quickly.

"Well, you already know the story. You don't want to hear it again."

"I do! I do! This is my favorite story in the world."

"Well, maybe it won't hurt to tell it one more time."

Back in those days, my little brother, Sammy, and I played cards in the evening. We liked to play a game called war, but we were not supposed to play it because that's what it turned into, and my mother was tired of listening to us fight.

Anyway, there we were in the kitchen, at the table, when Tornado came up and poked my leg. He did that when he wanted my attention, to remind me his dish was empty or something.

But there was food in his dish, and there was water in his bowl.

14

"You got everything you need. Stop poking me."

I went back to the card game, but Tornado poked me again.

"It's too dark to go for a walk," I said.

He poked me again.

I said to Sammy, "If I didn't know better, I'd think Tornado wants to play cards!"

Sammy said, "Then play cards with him. I'm tired of this stupid game."

Because he was losing, Sammy threw down his cards and left the room.

I looked down at Tornado. "You want to play cards?" I asked.

Tornado looked at me. His ears came forward as if he were inter-ested. I held the cards so he could see them. His ears came forward some more. I shuffled the cards. Now his ears were almost over his eyes.

"You want to play cards? Cards?"

I held out the deck. He waited. I fanned out the deck. He waited. I could see he was ready, willing, and able. He had that look he got when I had a ball and he was waiting for me to throw it.

Then I had an idea. I put one card out farther than the rest. "Pick a card, Tornado," I said. "Pick any card you want."

Tornado took one step forward. He stretched out his neck. He took the card. *He took the card!* I remember it to this day. It was the three of hearts. The dog was standing there with the three of hearts in his mouth!

Tornado stood there.

I sat there.

We waited.

The trouble was I didn't know what we were waiting for. I had a dog with the three of hearts in his mouth, a dog who could do a card trick, but I didn't know what the trick was.

"Put it back," I said, offering him the deck.

He didn't move. I tried to take the card from him and put it back myself, but he would not let go.

My daddy came in the kitchen for a glass of buttermilk. I said, "Daddy, Tornado knows a card trick!"

"Does he?"

"At least I think he does. Well, he knows half of a card trick."

"Half a card trick's better than none."

"See, I held out the cards like this,

and he took one, but now he won't let it go."

"Tornado, drop it!" my daddy commanded.

Tornado dropped the card and wagged his tail.

"Good dog," my daddy said.

"Daddy, do you want to see the card trick? I think I can do it now."

"If it doesn't take too long. I want to hear the news."

I put the card back in the deck. It didn't want to go because it was wet now and there were teeth marks in it.

"Pick a card, Tornado, any card," I said.

Tornado picked a card. I crossed my fingers for luck. "Tornado, if that card is the three of hearts, drop it!"

Tornado waited.

"Drop it!" my daddy ordered.

Tornado dropped the three of hearts.

"Good dog," I said. I felt really proud. I had a dog who could do a card trick, even though my daddy had to help.

"Is that it?" my daddy said.

"Yes, sir. You can get back to the news."

"The news can wait. Let's try that trick again."

CHAPTER 4
Carey's Turtle

"**T**elling that story always puts me in mind of the turtle."

"Turtle? You never told us about a turtle."

"Didn't I? Surely I told you about the turtle."

"No, you didn't, did he?"

"No," said my brother.

I said, "Was it your turtle?" to get him started. It worked.

Pete smiled.

───────

As I recall it, the turtle belonged to a girl named Carey, and it was about the size of a silver dollar.

My sister, Emma Lou, was looking after the turtle, and I mean she was particular about it—gave it fresh water every day whether the turtle wanted it or not, and wouldn't let any of us so much as near it.

One nice sunny day Emma Lou changed the water as usual and put the bowl out on the porch so the turtle could get some sun.

An hour went by. When Emma Lou went out again, the turtle was gone. You never heard such carrying on.

"Who took Carey's turtle? Mama, somebody stole Carey's turtle!"

I expect you could have heard her all over the county.

My brother and I swore up and down we hadn't done it, but Emma Lou didn't believe us.

"Mama, make them tell me what they did with Carey's turtle. I know they stole Carey's turtle."

My mother had come out to referee, and was giving my brother and me a little talking-to about playing jokes on people, when I looked over and saw Tornado.

Tornado was sitting by the steps, and he had a look on his face like something was wrong.

I went over to him, and I noticed that his mouth wasn't closed all the way. I pulled up his lip and saw a turtle foot.

I closed the lip back up quick as I could, because I didn't know whether the turtle was alive or dead, but my brother had already seen it too and said, "The turtle's in Tornado's mouth. I saw its foot." He was glad to be innocent for once.

I knew right away what had happened. Tornado had come around the house, seen the nice bowl of water, leaned down for a drink, and ended up with a mouthful of turtle.

Emma Lou came over and held out her hand. "Tornado, give me Carey's turtle. And that turtle better be all right or you'll be sorry."

Tornado just sat there, looking more troubled than ever.

"Tornado, I mean it. Give me that turtle!"

Tornado didn't move.

"Tornado, if you don't give me that turtle right this minute—"

I didn't let her finish. I said in

my father's voice, "Drop it!"

Tornado opened his mouth, and the turtle dropped into Emma Lou's hand. That turtle was good as new.

As soon as he dropped the turtle, Tornado went wild. He started running around the yard and around the barn and around the house. Sitting there for an hour with a turtle in his mouth and not knowing what to do with it must have been the worst thing that could happen to a dog. The only thing to do was run it off.

Well, it was catching. I started running along with him. Tornado would run around the tree one way and I'd run the other, and when we would almost bump into each other, it would make us run some more.

I don't know how long we kept it up, but finally we did bump into each other and just fell down on the ground.

"Good dog," I said when I got my breath back.

"Good dog?" Emma Lou said from the porch. "For lapping up Carey's turtle?"

"For keeping it safe," I reminded her.

"Oh, all right," she admitted. "Good dog."

CHAPTER 5
Five-Thirty

The wind was still howling, and we could hear the porch swing pounding the side of the house. Something like a tree branch hit the cellar doors.

Pete said, "One more quick story about Tornado."

"Not too quick," I said. "I like all the details."

I think he winked at me.

My sister, Emma Lou, had a cat. Its name was Five-Thirty.

It got the name because the cat used to come to our house every day at five-thirty to get something to eat. We didn't know where the cat came from, but it would jump up on the windowsill, and my mother would say, "Well, it must be five-thirty; here's the cat."

Pretty soon, my sister claimed the cat was hers. She tried to change the name to Silver Queen, for the kind of corn my daddy grew. She called the cat Queenie, but the cat was Five-Thirty to the rest of us.

Before Five-Thirty came along, we had a part-collie named Babe who liked to dig holes anywhere and anytime she felt like it. If she was in the house when the mood hit her, she'd try to dig a hole in the carpet.

Now Tornado was not a dog to go

around digging for the pure pleasure of digging. If he dug a hole, it was because he needed it. He took a lot of pride in the holes he dug.

One hot day, Tornado felt the need, and he went in the shade of those cut-off pine trees and dug a hole just the right size to lie in. And that's what he did.

After that, in the heat of the day, he would go lie down in the hole and relax. He got it right the first time, like he did most things, and never had to dig again.

Well, one hot day he went out to lie down, and there was Five-Thirty in the hole. She was licking a little loose dirt off one paw.

Five-Thirty looked at Tornado. Tornado looked at Five-Thirty. Five-Thirty yawned.

Tornado made a sound deep down in his throat that said, "Get out, please." Then he made another deeper sound that said, "Get out."

Five-Thirty did not budge. I would have tried to pick her up, but the cat didn't let anybody touch her but Emma Lou. I had scratches on my arms to prove it.

I started walking to the pond and called Tornado to follow me. He stayed where he was. I called him to the barn. He didn't budge.

He stayed right there looking at that cat in that hole until—you guessed it—five-thirty came around. Then the cat got up, yawned, stretched, and went to the house.

Tornado got in the hole, but not to lie down. He got in there to dig. He dug and he dug and he dug some more. Dirt flew everywhere.

I knew what he was doing—he was trying to get the feel and the smell and the memory of that cat out of his special place. And I knew he couldn't. Even if he dug all the way to China—and he was already twelve inches on the way—when he got there, it would still be Five-Thirty.

"Stop that dog," my mother cried from the kitchen window. "What's gotten into him?"

"Five-Thirty," I called back.

"I didn't ask the time," she called. "Get that dog out of there, and fill that hole in."

I did what she told me. I knew I was doing Tornado a favor, but he didn't see it that way. I pulled him out by the collar and locked him in the shed. He struggled a lot on the way there, and he barked the whole time I was shoveling the dirt back in the hole.

He took the loss of his lying-down hole hard. He never, to my knowledge, went in the pine trees again. Not even when we went in there to cut our Christmas tree—our half of a Christmas tree, I might say.

As far as I know, Tornado never dug another hole. And every time Five-Thirty came around, he looked the other way.

CHAPTER 6
Buddy

Pete opened the cellar doors. We peered around him, but my mother turned her head away, as if she didn't want to see.

There was hail lying on the ground and broken limbs and leaves everywhere.

"No real damage," Pete called to my mother in a cheerful voice.

My mother folded her hands over her heart.

"But I still don't like the look of

that sky," Pete said. "We better sit tight."

He closed the door and sat down.

"Do you remember anything else about Tornado?" I prompted.

"I remember one time. This was the saddest day of my life. I hate to tell it."

"Please," I said.

Well, my daddy and I went to town in the truck. Tornado was in the back. We hadn't planned on taking him, but as soon as my daddy lowered the tailgate, he jumped in like he knew what he was doing, so he got to go.

My daddy and I parked the truck on the side of the street and went in the hardware store. Tornado stayed behind in the truck.

We were gone about an hour. When we came back, my dad was loaded down with things, and I was carrying some paper bags filled with different sizes of nails.

As we got closer to the truck, I heard a voice saying, "It's Buddy! It's Buddy!" in an excited way. "Mama, Papa, it's Buddy. Oh, Buddy, Buddy! I never thought I'd see you again. Buddy!"

There was a family standing around the back of our truck, and one of the girls had climbed in. She had thrown her arms around Tornado's neck. She was the one saying all the *Buddy*s.

I stopped where I was. To save my life, I couldn't have taken another step. The bags of nails fell from my hands onto the sidewalk. It was as

if they nailed me down.

My daddy shifted his packages to rest a hand on my shoulder. He had warned me not to get too fond of the dog. "He's not yours yet," he had said over and over again, but both my parents had asked around and nobody knew who he belonged to.

Well I had got fond of him—more than fond. I loved the dog. He was mine. And now some girl was calling him *Buddy*.

My daddy held my shoulder tighter and said, "What's going on?" to a short man in suspenders.

"Is this your truck?" the man asked.

"It is."

"This dog," the man said, "looks exactly like our dog, Buddy, that got blown away in the August tornado."

"That's about when we found him," my daddy admitted. "He came to us. He was in our yard."

I had stopped breathing. Everybody had, except the short man in the suspenders.

"My girl carried on something awful when she found that dog was gone. She's always been real fond of him. Her grandfather gave him to her."

"My boy's gotten fond of the dog too," my daddy said.

There was a long and terrible silence. Then the man in the suspenders said, "Well, maybe I better go get the police or something to settle this."

"That won't be necessary," my daddy said. "You take the dog. He's rightfully yours."

They let down the tailgate and

took Tornado out of the back of our truck. They loaded him into theirs. Tornado didn't look real happy, but I couldn't do a thing to stop what was happening. I was still nailed to the concrete.

My daddy put his packages in the truck and came back and picked up my nails for me.

"Let's go home, Petey," he said, using the name he called me when I was little. Then he fell silent. Even my daddy couldn't find the good in this.

The truck was pulling away from the curb. Tornado was in the back.

I tried to get one last look at my dog, but my eyes were too full of tears.

If my daddy had not helped me into the truck, I'd be standing there to this day.

CHAPTER 7

The End of the Storm

Pete paused to wipe his eyes. That story always made him cry. It made me cry too. I wiped my eyes on my arm and then wiped my arm on my shirt.

"Go on," I urged.

He took a deep breath to help himself continue.

That day, that miserable Saturday, was the saddest, longest day of my life. I couldn't eat. I did my chores without knowing I was doing them. I couldn't play cards after supper. I couldn't sleep. There was an emptiness about my room that matched the one inside me. The whole house seemed empty—the whole outdoors—the whole world.

I didn't go around exactly boo-hooing, but my eyes kept filling up with tears. As soon as I'd wipe one flood away, another would come. I felt like it would be that way for the rest of my life.

Sunday passed the same lonely way. Then Monday and Tuesday. On Wednesday, my mother got tired of what she called my moping, and she took me aside to talk some sense into me.

"You knew you might lose the dog," she said.

I nodded.

"You knew he wasn't yours."

I nodded.

"You've got to stop moping around. You're going to make yourself sick."

I nodded. I felt like I already was.

"Listen. We can get another dog. There are other dogs in the county."

I shook my head back and forth. "Not for me."

On Friday I was in the barn, and I heard a thumping sound. It was the sound that Tornado's tail used to make against the barn door when he wanted to come inside.

My eyes flooded. I couldn't help it. I knew there was no thumping. It was a sound I wanted to hear so bad, my ears just heard it. There wasn't any thumping. There couldn't be.

But the thumping went on, and it

really was thumping. It got faster.

I wiped my eyes and I looked, and Tornado was standing in the doorway. My Tornado was standing in the doorway!

"Tornado's back!" I yelled. "Tornado, good boy, good boy!"

I threw my arms around him. He curved his body the way he did when he was pleased about something, and his tail wagged in my face.

My daddy came to the door. "Tornado's back!" I told him.

"So I see."

"We don't have to take him back to those people, do we?" I tightened my hold on Tornado's neck.

"Well, I don't rightly know how we could," my daddy said. "The man wasn't polite enough to give us his name."

"That's true."

"And if they find us, well, the dog knows where we are. He can come over for a visit anytime he takes a mind to."

"Yes, but I want him to stay."

"I do too," my daddy said, "but if we have to share him with other folks, we'll do it. Half a Tornado is better than none."

And my father and I laughed.

There was a long pause in the cellar. I asked, "Did he stay?" I like a good ending.

"For seven happy years," Pete said.

"And the people never came and got him?"

"No. Course we didn't make the mistake of taking him to town again."

Pete stood up, took off his hat, and put it back on his head. He stretched. "I'm going to take another look outside."

But before he could open the doors, there was a loud knock.

"Hello in there! Anybody home?"

It was my father's voice.

"Storm's over!" he cried.

We rushed out through the cellar doors and into the fresh air. My mother hugged my daddy. "Oh, Link, I was worried."

As soon as my grandmother got up the steps, she hugged him too. Then she gave him a stern look and said, "Lincoln, I hope you had the good sense to get in a ditch."

"Look at me, Mama, can't you tell? Don't anybody else hug me. I'm too muddy to hug."

My little brother hung back to speak to Pete. "Could Tornado really and truly do a card trick?"

"He could."

"And did you really and truly have a cat named Five-Thirty?"

"We did."

My older brother said, "I wish you had told the story about Tornado and the rooster. That's my favorite."

"Next time," Pete promised. Then he winked at me. "If there is one."

Also by Betsy Byars . . .

The Pinballs

Three unwanted kids collide in a foster home and learn to depend on each other.

ALA Notable Book
Bank Street Children's Book Award
SLJ Best Book

Pb 0-06-440198-7

Me Tarzan

There's no controlling Dorothy when she practices her Tarzan yell. When the circus and the school play open on the same night, things get wild!

Hc 0-06-028706-3
Pb 0-06-442119-8

The Seven Treasure Hunts

Jackson and his scheming friend Goat set up treasure hunts for each other, but they find a lot more trouble than treasure!

Pb 0-06-440435-8

HarperTrophy®
An Imprint of HarperCollinsPublishers
www.harperchildrens.com
www.betsybyars.com